A DIFFERENT WOLF

THE HUGH MACLENNAN POETRY SERIES

Editors: Allan Hepburn and Carolyn Smart

Titles in the series
Waterglass Jeffery Donaldson
All the God-Sized Fruit Shawna Lemay
Chess Pieces David Solway
Giving My Body to Science Rachel Rose
The Asparagus Feast S.P. Zitner
The Thin Smoke of the Heart Tim Bowling
What Really Matters Thomas O'Grady
A Dream of Sulphur Aurian Haller
Credo Carmine Starnino
Her Festival Clothes Mavis Jones
The Afterlife of Trees Brian Bartlett
Before We Had Words S.P. Zitner
Bamboo Church Ricardo Sternberg
Franklin's Passage David Solway
The Ishtar Gate Diana Brebner
Hurt Thyself Andrew Steinmetz
The Silver Palace Restaurant Mark Abley
Wet Apples, White Blood Naomi Guttman
Palilalia Jeffery Donaldson
Mosaic Orpheus Peter Dale Scott
Cast from Bells Suzanne Hancock
Blindfold John Mikhail Asfour
Particles Michael Penny
A Lovely Gutting Robin Durnford
The Little Yellow House Heather Simeney MacLeod
Wavelengths of Your Song Eleonore Schönmaier
But for Now Gordon Johnston
Some Dance Ricardo Sternberg

Outside, Inside Michael Penny
The Winter Count Dilys Leman
Tablature Bruce Whiteman
Trio Sarah Tolmie
hook nancy viva davis halifax
Where We Live John Reibetanz
The Unlit Path Behind the House Margo Wheaton
Small Fires Kelly Norah Drukker
Knots Edward Carson
The Rules of the Kingdom Julie Paul
Dust Blown Side of the Journey Eleonore Schönmaier
slow war Benjamin Hertwig
The Art of Dying Sarah Tolmie
Short Histories of Light Aidan Chafe
On High Neil Surkan
Translating Air Kath MacLean
The Night Chorus Harold Hoefle
Look Here Look Away Look Again Edward Carson
Delivering the News Thomas O'Grady
Grotesque Tenderness Daniel Cowper
Rail Miranda Pearson
Ganymede's Dog John Emil Vincent
The Danger Model Madelaine Caritas Longman
A Different Wolf Deborah-Anne Tunney

A Different Wolf

Deborah-Anne Tunney

McGill-Queen's University Press
Montreal & Kingston • London • Chicago

ISBN 978-0-2280-0182-9 (paper)
ISBN 978-0-2280-0315-1 (ePDF)
ISBN 978-0-2280-0316-8 (ePUB)

Legal deposit second quarter 2020
Bibliothèque nationale du Québec

Printed in Canada on acid-free paper that is 100% ancient forest free
(100% post-consumer recycled), processed chlorine free

Financé par le gouvernement du Canada — Funded by the Government of Canada Conseil des arts du Canada — Canada Council for the Arts

We acknowledge the support of the Canada Council for the Arts.

Nous remercions le Conseil des arts du Canada de son soutien.

Library and Archives Canada Cataloguing in Publication

Title: A different wolf/Deborah-Anne Tunney.

Names: Tunney, Deborah-Anne, author.

Series: Hugh MacLennan poetry series.

Description: Series statement: Hugh MacLennan poetry series

Identifiers: Canadiana (print) 20200175386 | Canadiana (eBOOK) 20200175440 | ISBN 9780228001829 (paper) | ISBN 9780228003151 (ePDF) | ISBN 9780228003168 (ePUB)

Classification: LCC PS8639.U56 D54 2020 | DDC C811/.6—dc23

This book was typeset by Marquis Interscript in 9.5/13 Sabon.

To Matthew,
fellow lover of Hitchcock

CONTENTS

Bel Air, 1980   3

WOMAN IN THE MALE GAZE

Melanie at the Birthday Party   7
Carnival   8
Carlotta   9
The Women's Washroom   10
Madeleine, Dear Madeleine   11
To Catch a Thief with Grace   12
The Redwoods Bear Witness   13
Crows   14
Oak Room, NYC   15
Marion, Lost   16
Cube   17
The Remake   18
The Unnamed Wife   19
Devlin and Alicia   20
Psycho   21
Dial M   22
The Stage   23
Torture the Woman   24
Tippi and Suzanne   25
Annie and Melanie   26
Death in the Foyer   27

INNOCENCE AND GUILT

Shadows and Doubt   31
Roped-in   32
How Foolish   33
Boat Life   34
Frenzied   35
The Next Morning   36
Drive-in   37
Notoriety   38
The Uses of Suspense   39
Watching *Lifeboat*   40
Hero   41
Charlie and Charlie   42
Judy, the Heartbroken   43
Psycho, Again   44
Spiral   45
Watching   46
Visitor   47
Dialing M   48
What Lydia Finds   49
Midge at Home   50
July 1952   51

TIME AND DEATH

Visitation   55
Watching *Vertigo*   56
Drive-in, 1969   57
NbyNW   58
1945/1965   59
The Eternal Child   60
Birds   62
On the Cusp   63

A Story of the London Fog   64
Life on That Boat   65
The View from Point Reyes   66
Torn Curtain   67
Bodega Bay, 2012   68
Old Mission, San Juan Bautista   69
The Man Who Thought He Knew Too Much   70
Canada as Backdrop   71
Spellbinding   72
Santa Rosa, 1943   73
The Back Lot   74
Alma and Alfred   75
This Is All True   76

The Wolf in the Basement   79

Notes and Acknowledgments   81

A DIFFERENT WOLF

Nothing has changed since Little Red Riding Hood faced the big bad wolf. What frightens us today is exactly the same sort of thing that frightened us yesterday. It's just a different wolf.

Alfred Hitchcock

BEL AIR, 1980

On these days, Hitch, when you are old
and slowly dying in Bel Air, the view of
the golf course out your window – what do
you remember? Clarinet jazz in jewelled
rooms with women drowsy from romance
their beauty against the cool turquoise of night –
or is it the conjuring of shorelines
alleyways, graveyards? – a sky heavy with navy

you lean back into this settled moment
and think of her, the way the future
held no surprise until you heard her laugh
saw the sway of her blonde hair, the walk
away from you in high heels –
she was love in another place
in the sun, on a beach, and you followed
like the sick dog your heart
was – wanting and barking and wanting.

WOMAN IN THE MALE GAZE

Blondes make the best victims. They're like virgin snow that shows up the bloody footprints.

Alfred Hitchcock

MELANIE AT THE BIRTHDAY PARTY

steps down the steep path into the yard, where children
play and balloons dip, as sudden tyrants of hate darken the sky

on the windy patio the birthday party whirls, the smell
of ocean air over the children's cries, their blindfolded quest

evening invades in even threads of time; beyond the emerging
dark and night's cool sapphire silk, the tattered birds wait –

identical lumps, each a handful of black pulsing, the chorus
line receding into an intricate distance. their screech settles
    inside her.

bracelets of claws, pearls of malice: treacherous as stilettos.
                                        The Birds, 1963

CARNIVAL

this world of Ferris wheels, lit
against the sky, a circling geometry
the crowd beneath holds pink
beehives of candy floss, munching peanuts, pretzels

trash litters the fairway –
and it is here we find him, bursting
the child's balloon with a cigarette, stalking
the trio into the crazed tunnel of
love

her death in the abandoned glasses
placid double screen, watching –
the grass where her body falls
accepts the weight, its inevitability
this is the pivot from which he will not return –

how still that moment when she arched back into the cool
night, her summer death – how easy
it was to squeeze her life away – that surprised him –
that and the way he could never
forgive himself.

Strangers on a Train, 1951

CARLOTTA

He follows her to the vacant church, through
the nave into the Romanesque
courtyard where sun blanches tombstones, he
follows to the polished hotel, heavy
with furniture and the past

her perfume coaxes like brilliant light

wounds the retina: the yellow the pink the mauve blossoms
against a shadowed sky glows ephemeral –

and the sweep of her hair, a series of blonde stars –
even the street he cruises is platinum with quiet

while her pink blush, sparked bloom contrasts
with his solemn survey and collapses under the fist
of his black longing

Vertigo, 1958

She stands in the diagonal shadow
of the closed stall, listening to the nonsense
of the women clamouring by the mirror, like birds
clamour by an open window, and then
silence, proof of her aloneness –
when she's sure no one can see
she moves back to the office, her fingers clever as an abacus
while beside her the dim, deaf woman cleans
with her back to the crime

this woman wants to finish early, her thoughts
are of the family she feeds, a television on
in the living room, the sun between curtains
moving across an improvised sky – she does
not hear the drop of the shoe, for she
cannot conceive of Marnie, of the solid rooms
where she hides, where the mother
reigns, rubbing her damaged leg, and the sky
outside pushes down, crimson with disapproval

Marnie, 1964

MADELEINE, DEAR MADELEINE

The first time he saw her she was leaving the rococo room
on her husband's arm, the simple sweep of her pearly hair
her grey eyes looking beyond him –

he sat at the bar with his back to the room
his sideways glance, his hand around a glass
of whisky, the music swelling behind her

the first time he saw her something shattered, so that her
gliding past him, like a yacht in sunlight, was really
his life draining away from him, was really the moment
when all he believed became bleached into pain
caught in a graveyard of loose light, a pierce
to his unyielding, unknowable heart.

Vertigo, 1958

Her sports car speeds along the Promenade
des Anglais, hugging the bay of Nice
it climbs ever higher into a dangerous
future; her blonde hair whips
behind her, her clever face polished as chrome
in the early afternoon light
of another Mediterranean day –

these moments of freedom
before the marriage, the children on the beach
before the accident along that very highway
resonate forever, moments trapped on film
its own form of memory, prove life can be pure
and cool as her fingertips on his cheek
as flawless as the sky over the bay, misty
indeterminate, and stuck in its blue time

To Catch a Thief, 1955

The crash of waves held in his
mind as he bends her head
back, locks her in a kiss

love, like light, illuminates her fake face

Vertigo, 1958

CROWS

Feathered fists, baubles on a branch, a string of black onyx
sway in the cool breeze of a California
spring – a twittering nuisance or a message? your

choice, Hitch – contemplating, your numb face
hangs bland, lips heavy, flesh loose, twined
and sinewy, and plain ugly, and in this mass
a tiny, ticking knowing – how the sun rises

and the shore blooms before you, like women walking
along a corridor, the architect that keeps you
chained, your heavy grin pulling the rubbery lips back
a skull too large, the hair a dull mass, cut close
while eyes dart trapped in doughy flesh
and always ravenous

The Birds, 1963

OAK ROOM, NYC

I drank in that bar, across from the park, the very one
with the murky painting of horses and some Parisian scene
of manners and speculations, and could that be a dancing bear?
there he was, sitting with the men, refugees from the office
buildings that crowded the sky outside the Georgian windows.
I was a tourist and alert when the night settled, the dark
shooed away by the gold-yellow lamps that made velvet
the light falling on the evening, the wine ruby and warm
on my tongue, and I thought of him, the victim, the well-dressed
fool, ushered into limousines at gunpoint, thought of how he
never made it back to those rooms with their smoky
men-in-bar feel, he became lost in mansions instead
in the train's urge forward, alone in that huge cornfield while
the warning of that wayward plane, like the future, bore down
                              North by Northwest, 1959

you took a wrong turn, back there
off the main highway, globes
of smeared light above you
receding planets, you left behind
that office, your pressed pencil
skirt and clever blouse
buttoned and secretarial.

somewhere along the highway
the scenery sullied,
the rain came, traffic glare
washed your face, so that you
squinted and turned away –
it was heartbreaking to watch
your tender need.

do I have to see this again? I think
watching you stand in the roadside
washroom, counting the money
as I hover above you
like the angel you so desperately need.

Psycho, 1960

CUBE

Like Melanie in her telephone booth, we
are all caught in our glass cubes
our hands splayed on the cracked window –
we have all been forced into the wild
carnage of that fire-rimmed street, and who
will rescue us? Who'd risk all to fold
that door in and pull us
out, take us back to that room
with the cowering villagers, their
faces now raw with fear and
stupidity, standing in their circle
of communal blame – the slap rings true, as

birds amass on high drifts of air, black
laughter darkening their vast outstretch of wings

The Birds, 1963

THE REMAKE

He remade her in the gauzy
neon light caught in the

sheer curtain, a dreamy conspiracy of
mood and mirrors full of fogged memories

She rose from her Midwest ambition into
the blonde luminance of a California shoreline

And in her heart was treachery
of the most serene sort

He remade her and dragged her into the vacant
tower, pearly evening light spreading over the fields

spreading like early morning mist, far below them
obscuring, redemptive

Vertigo, 1958

THE UNNAMED WIFE

Fogged pathway, cliffed escarpment, danger flies
up like birds in sudden flight, and her delicate step
slips on the leaves' muddy palms – she stops, listens
in the gloaming hour, to the tide she cannot see

Her husband beside her, closed off –
he's been here before, with another wife
a woman with thorned hair that
grew into vines entwining Manderley
leaving a mystery of tresses

What does his watchfulness tell her –
the way he looks into the dim, invisible distance
his glance away from her into a private corridor
simmering in the past, the air perfumed
now with the malfeasance of Rebecca's memory –

there remains yet the prison hood
of the unnamed wife's vision, the dominance of her rival's
legacy, and the winter at the heart of their love

Rebecca, 1940

DEVLIN AND ALICIA

Starting as intrigue, it moves
to the place where romance is suspense
old men stand like sentinels guarding
the threshold, hunched in their plans
for dominance

She is tested again and again, fails
fidelity, that red rose
her past an ugliness that hides
the virginal longings, and how
she yearns for rescue

leans back into that black marriage
while in her mind is want of the cruelest sort –
it's the thing that tells her
how young she is and
tells us how damaged

Notorious, 1946

PSYCHO

The silk slip: your idea of sin? your idea
of redemption: her death in a hotel, off
the main highway, a 1950 rain falling, the breeze
moving into the sad room, the curtain a wave of
time. Women wore high heels then, my mother, for example.
I remember them kicked beneath the chesterfield when
she'd return from work – her death was not a mystery
it was sordid and prolonged and more terrifying than that dithering
murderer at the window, looking down through the night at the rain
and used car, and her blonde stupid head.

Psycho, 1960

Nothing as mundane as meals –
no oven, refrigerator, we never see
the kitchen

But there are appetites

And there is a living room
where they are stuck, a bedroom
in wait, and there are strategies
a cart for the alcohol, the colour of urine
(or is it honey?) in cut crystal
with which he plies
the dispensable fool

The men mere artifact to her, they
orbit her passive beauty, wrestle it to grey, and
by the end stand stage still, encased in the stiff
corset of their blind roles

Dial M for Murder, 1954

Here we are in the living room
with Melanie and Mitch
and Mitch's mother, and his sister, Cathy
Here's the piano, the
dining room table, here's the
kitchen where Mitch and his
mother discuss Melanie –
her waywardness – while a string
of black birds like a string of black
pearls perch on the wires
each skull shines
tiny black moons

And here we are again, in the living
room, waiting for the attack –
silence lengthens into the
sky, down to the bay
out to the ocean, and now
the birds, their thousand voices
enter through the fireplace
their clamouring, a form of love

The Birds, 1963

His wife's delicate mind shredded to rags
ripped fabric, she darkens at the edge
as the plot veers into injustice

By the end she's held captive
strict in a straight chair
staring at the corner and can
not unstick her gaze

Simple thoughts clamoured for
release: the iron frying pan each
morning where bacon sizzled and
the sad, bulging eyes of his

eggs were rimmed by burnt lace
their children's laugh an evil now
her pain part of the equation
the accusation, that leaves
him alone with his guilt

The Wrong Man, 1956

You got something right in that scene, the tone
of conspiracy, the lean to understand, the
volley of sympathy – they could be friends
in another setting

This blonde and brunette, on either side
of the room, on either side of your
desire.   You used the resignation
of Annie, the privilege of Melanie
as ideals and let them peck out their
place on the high wire

After the phone call, the knock of
that bird's death, the perfect profiles
that turn to the full moon, luxuriate in its light
and promise that moves out beyond the dusty
road, spirals high above the Bay's
restless waves

The Birds, 1963

ANNIE AND MELANIE

A cool California night, a night
when you may need a throw, she
lights a cigarette and settles into the living room
chair, to listen to the story of how Annie

ended up there, alone in that bungalow, off
a dirt road, speaking of the shacks on a hillside
of Lydia with her mind shaped like a
kitchen, the crazed cruel love Annie

keeps hidden in a cupboard, between
them the phone conversation, and Annie
leans back into pain, a certainty rising
before her like another wicked day

like the sun that burns enormous, its
scorch round and solid and full of someone else's joy

The Birds, 1963

Pulled down into the floating drape
of her purple gown
the foyer huge as a militaristic sky

Her hair, a long cascade, thrown back
her neck snaps, and she stares in
awe, awfully, at the ceiling, at its gold
filigree where stories of loss are locked
and there they stay, imprisoned in a waltz
of purple blood, an orchid's bloom,
forlorn, her orphan death

Topaz, 1969

INNOCENCE AND GUILT

I have a feeling that inside you somewhere, there's somebody
nobody knows about.

Alfred Hitchcock

These are the things left behind: priscilla
curtains with sun caught in their sway
the kitchen off the back porch, the front yard
with marigolds rimming the walkway

The mother sleepwalks through his deception
the father ineffectual as a prop –
they see only the dark and light that comes
in deceiving cycles

while there in the corner, as if in a web
the murderer blows smoke rings that mutate
ghosts of the dead, the lamp on until
morning's silver gloom spreads over the chenille
on her princess bed, seething warm
in the room's lukewarm light

Shadow of a Doubt, 1943

In our first moments, we were shown only his last moment
the rope tightened around the neck
the slump that meant death, and
the taming of life into an equation of spite

left with the murderers: those silly boys
one breathing in the new scent
of his power, the other sulking as a sheer
greyness descended onto the cityscape

behind them, they moved into a landscape of mordancy
and debate while the props stood in a circle, talking:
the fated fiancée, flustered maid, complicit teacher
isolated in their roles – by the corpse

folded in the trunk, his life seeping
away without sound or hope, in the middle of everything

Rope, 1948

to let them all go, leaving you alone with the
murderer and the dark yard stuck in its resilient night

the sound of his approach like chains, like the dragging
of limbs, as if all the weight of his life was moving
   disembodied
toward you, automaton horrible, pathetic and dull-eyed

he says, *what do you want from me?*
his slack face heavy, a touch doltish

it's a good question though, for you are so full
of want, but then the flash of redemptive light
freezes him: a large, sad man, unloved by his wife

haunting the hallways of 3:00 a.m. with a suitcase
full of knives

Rear Window, 1954

Take one lifeboat, cram it with seven people, stuff the sky
with threatening clouds, strew the horizon with promise
of salvation in the form of a floating island of metal –
make the voyage in the midst of war, banish rooms
walls, and here it comes: the bad behaviour

drag out the theories of nature's redness, Hobbes's hell
and what remains? the raucous ranting
of the legless, the Nazi urge rowing on and on, the flowing
hair of Tallulah, wet and tangled, caught in the twist of his dirty
fist, her laugh lost to the hysteria of their raised voices –
rowdy animals tumble over each other until
the calm of trust, the silence that betrays blooming
off stage, like welcome heat.

Lifeboat, 1944

FRENZIED

We part in the hallway outside the apartment
stay in his churning mind that drags
us down the staircase, through a muffled claustrophobia
that opens to the street –
listen: there's horns, the bustle of crowds
a bird's screech

We know what is happening
what chasm has opened wide
her epiphany and descent coincide

sacks of potatoes, lumpy
and dusted with earth hold
the naked girl, her dead, dirty feet in
his dirty, dead mind.

Poetic, he thinks, until the pin stabs its fear
in a single shard of light, pierces deep and sharp
and what is human in him retreats.

Frenzy, 1972

When he woke, something was different
the air thinner, the courtyard closed in

The window was an eye that would not shut
it fed him the world in screens: the ponytailed dancer
the musician hunched over his piano

The lit cigarette in the dark with
the murderer coiled behind its orange O

nothing would ever again be as interesting to him

not even his final plummet into the garden
with the stone path rushing up to meet him
and then those faces crowding down
like petals in a giant flower

after the crack of bone hits
cement – a new fierce fact
hitting the heart.

Rear Window, 1954

White rectangle leans against the dimming sky
amid the desolation of a darkening day, the seaside
town appears, the bay's clumped grey clouds, her
stiletto walk along the wharf – while behind me boys
jostle each other, smoke up and – oh, how we laugh
as the night comes in and the huge image of that living
room looms before us – how raw we are in our new
bodies that stretch away into the tempered night

We're silent watching the mother venture into
the back hall, past the chipped teacups into the bedroom
the bird stuck in the window pane, the body, sad in
pyjamas, lies splayed on the floor, in the
corner: close,

                    closer,

                          closest

to the burnt hollowed sockets – her purse, full of dread
thuds behind her – the night is made of silk now, it moves
over us like a cool wave. The dark the screen is propped
against is solid as the past, we laugh and the sounds
fragment into the sky where caws coalesce

The Birds, 1963

Loved by two men
and no wonder, her beauty, a commodity
each man cruel in his own way
each man twisting the thick
braid of that beauty to his will

Her hand where the key burns
an outline opens
to cup his fevered cheek, the bend back
into delirium from the truth of their
kiss, and always the misguided
trust that leaves her bedridden, hidden

in an upstairs room, the
mother-in-law's Nazi bulk
in the doorway and later still
the husband stoops, freeing
her to her next imprisonment

Notorious, 1946

Oh come now, he can't die, and what of the puppy?
Or the woman holding him in her purse?
Blown to smithereens?
Left as charred bodies on the street
with parts of the bus, the street lamps
with curious onlookers looking on
What was all that suspense for? Mere tragedy?

There's something wrong here
all this death, the stupidity of her husband
the laughing knives –
There they all go, swept away in a flurry of fire
and police whistles, and sirens, except
the lovers, except for love that always
descends and leaves all in tatters
in mystery and meaning

Sabotage, 1936

It's meaning I'm after, settling down this winter afternoon
to watch, the day grows around me like a shell hardens
it's utter grey, and the sky palely, continuously grey. it seeps
into me, dulling as those images dull with their celluloid
claustrophobia. death settles, as the mist with its scent
of forever settles, so that I am lulled by the peace of hope's
diminishment. until the horizon grows wide with warring
ships, and the clamouring cacophony of voices from that litter
of rollicking animals is quieted before the German future
rushing at them, before the entrapment of their tiny souls in
their tiny vessels, hungry for some shape of love and unsure
if the wet on their cheek is from a kiss or from spit

Lifeboat, 1944

HERO

The field, a taut vastness, darker at the horizon
a tendon of stretched cloud quivering in the afternoon
heat: two men in suits by a cornfield face each other

The hero watches the interloper like a fox watches prey
some propriety keeps him on his side, the formality
of the road between them perhaps, its dusty silence

When he crosses over, the man points out the crop
duster then boards the chrome bus – alone now, except
for the plane, plump in the sky, gathering speed

It's always about death and escaping it, it's what a hero
does – it's about bringing us into that field, under a sky
of continuous distance, stilling our minds, so we contemplate

The blunt featurelessness of death, how it is without plot or
scenery or sense – so that there's relief when next we land
in the lobby of a Chicago hotel watching the woman

In her fiery dress search the paper for word of his death.
North by Northwest, 1959

CHARLIE AND CHARLIE

To kill Charlie would have been to kill himself, the small
boy he had been, loved so by his big sister

The tracks blurring while he waited for the right
moment, and she, struck with horror – or was it

awe? – in his arms. This was the moment when she
tore the front door off his façade and saw the

tailored swine lurking within. Here in the hooded
chase, his animal intensity, there was

nothing else he could do but die, so the day would
return to the church world opening up to gardens

caught in the catholic bloom of a sunny graveyard
                                    Shadow of a Doubt, 1943

JUDY, THE HEARTBROKEN

Oh, Scottie, do you not know me?
look at the stray you have become
roaming the lost streets
the scent of that blonde woman once
on your fingers, radiating off me, green
as my mawkish dress, the silly pearls

and if I do become her again, if I fade
into her platinum omnipotence, shimmering in
the green light of your obsession,
will you forget her and love me then?

Oh, Scottie, do not speak, put your hand there,
your mouth here, oh, foolish Scottie,
do you not recognize me now?

Vertigo, 1958

PSYCHO, AGAIN

The same hotel room, the same talk of
alimony, the hardware store in Fairvale, the
snap shut of her purse clasp, a period at
the end of a sentence. the end of their
affair – the last time he'll see her

Now here are the birds caught in frantic
flight, frozen above the room where she
sits, eats sandwiches, and drinks milk. we know
she'll never see the dawn or her escape. we know

what is clutched in the talons of those birds –
what future presses down, we've been
here before, hoping for another outcome
a veer toward that porterhouse steak in

the dining room with her sister while a calm
evening plays out on the street and enters
their soiled lives like a clean spring breeze

Psycho, 1960

SPIRAL

It all leads to the moment on the spiral stairs
when we see him mounting each step carefully
and the camera swirls about the glowing glass

What is it he brings her? the accumulation
of their deceitful marriage? forgiveness
in the form of light?

And what if she's wrong? who would
he be if the suspicion proved false? a boy
stuffed in a husband suit, always
outsmarted by fate – destitute
and without a plan

How artless, for it is her sweet suspicion
that holds us there, listening to his ascent, hungry for
the threat of his competence, and mesmerized
by the utter white of that pretty poison

Suspicion, 1941

milky mist expands the passageway,
the graveside, it roams the bay; mouldy night erupts grey
touches the sea with inky dark, the enormous
tumultuous sky, churning its adult deceit

This is what stays with me: those numb hours
of watching, the ache behind his blue eyes
the flat silver tongue of hair, stuck in the
cage of his confining car, the flattened

distance blooms wide and false as he trails
her essence, something residue, smoke
from a cigarette perhaps, mesmerized
by the light, a brilliant ocean of time

I follow him again, then again: a form of sleep

Vertigo, 1958

VISITOR

She sees him first on the train platform
his fedora tilted; coat draped over his thieving shoulders
and a smile sharp as knives

Visitor: its etymology is the same as village
villain, the person from away, the vile other

She sees only his brightness, the emerald
star he places in her palm that burns
a scar in the widow's initials

From the alleys of crime he brought
his hours of smoky hatred, watching
the ruined ceilings of hotel rooms

as detectives watched from the street
his window growing gold against the night

Above, the moon a scythe, serrated arc and sharp
Shadow of a Doubt, 1943

There were no cloudy afternoons, no rainstorms
nothing to disturb the continuous room
where she was caught in her itchy red dress
mixing martinis and clipping coupons

Waiting for the pinch of truth
her neck already sore and chafed

Other rooms bloomed beside
the warring fates – rooms that were a
marriage or rooms that were the past –
enclosing us in the gloom of 1950 London

There's hardly any blood, he said of the dead man
on their rug; there's hardly any love either

Held in their role's tight attire, the rooms filled
with their amiable, evil talk, while
beyond the window, a staged silence listened

Dial M for Murder, 1951

WHAT LYDIA FINDS

Pale with regret, the morning light spreads
over the room, casts anemic shadows, sinks
into the mind's hidden region where thoughts
of death ferment – this light, stark as strands of illness
dropped from a forgotten sky, smoulders in the room's huge
silence, shows the pecked body, cornered

Outside, a simple day
shimmers in the fields, sun rests
on crops, lone flecks of birds like far
checkmarks scatter against the sky
locked in a sea of rambling blue

Such deceiving peace, ignored by the tug
of escape into her frantic truck
that kicks dust into the sunny day, not knowing who
she is now, or who they are, waiting
her return in the laneway, a man, a woman, images that sway
before her in the truck's windshield as she careens home

The Birds, 1963

Her apartment with the view of Lombard Street
and the white cluster of buildings along the hillside
here we find him, explaining the spinning world
to her, and his place in it.
The room is yellow, she wears a yellow sweater
and the sun so strong that shadows
mock their contrast

Gradually the world is to darken
she feels it in her bones, a new duplicity
grey and unyielding as the gravestones
he visits without her that first day
life became uncertain, soiled, leading
to the moment she walked the asylum hallway
brooding, and suddenly, ineluctably, old.

Vertigo, 1958

We were at a cottage on Constance Bay, and the night
of my birth my mother and father played cards
at the dining room table, the slap of the screen
door that led from the porch made them glance
up, tell my brother and sister to stop running. this
was the time I was thrown into – this, the family
my mother leaning on the restless circle of me
went back to the cards laid out before her

and on that night, you dined at the Chateau
Frontenac, drank a bottle of Chianti
later dreamed of alleyways, escarpments, skies
blocked by monsters of sooted cathedrals

This was what awaited that July night, when the loons
cast their long thin moan to summer, the cool from the
lake floated up to the cottage and touched her tender
skin, awakening the wide arc of my arrival, and you
the closest you would ever be to me, bent
in your pious labour, setting for eternity the silence
of crime on film, lonely men who genuflect
before the basilica's nave and were caught
in the vestry's catholic sunlight

I Confess, 1953

TIME AND DEATH

We seem to have a compulsion these days to bury time capsules in order to give those people living in the next century or so some idea of what we are like. I have prepared one of my own. I have placed some rather large samples of dynamite, gunpowder, and nitroglycerin. My time capsule is set to go off in the year 3000. It will show them what we are really like.

Alfred Hitchcock

VISITATION

On the street, the moon rises like a host before the chalice –
    landlady with
worry in her apron pocket sees the coils of money beneath
the bed rolling away like dust.

He speaks as if from a grave, the bed a coffin and he lying in
    wait, slow
with solemn speech, remembers Burman street all those years
    ago, how
his sister saw him blondly sweet, before the disease
flared forward, a fire captive in a bedroom closet, where he
    first

felt that serene hatred like clear-sightedness, before the snake
    tangle
in gowns, the waltz through the trash land of discarded life
smoke and light drape in curtains, awake with dread while
    the world sleeps blind

Shadow of a Doubt, 1943

WATCHING *VERTIGO*

I understand that evening out
the rear view window of the DeSoto
the bridge distant over his shoulder

I understand the silence of his car as he followed
her into cemeteries, alleyways, bars, where ice
jingled in tall glasses – stars would sound like that,
if stars sounded, the crystal ice of her voice

the isolated point of sound of her heel on concrete
the echo past the guards and priests
reverberating out to a fateful San Francisco sky

I know what it means: the fabric of his longing
the unfurling of waves pulling him out
like the moon pulls him free of his wrong yearnings
past the crags, into an eternity of blue and loss

Vertigo, 1958

DRIVE-IN, 1969

Watching the movie so many years later, this is what I think:
one night in the summer of my 17th year, at a drive-in with
Margo and Darlene and Jimmy, the air becoming thick silk,
cool on my bare arms as the sun went down, and we were
sitting in Jimmy's car, our feet on the dashboard, on the chair
backs, and this movie played on the screen. It was like a TV
being on in a living room; everyone spoke over it, threw
popcorn at each other, laughed and shouted to friends who
walked by, as we spun out the long, hilarious spool of our
teenage selves. But there was also something like ghosts in
the air, something coming, our adult versions perhaps, like
the birds that swooped down on the serene seaside town, and
on this night, before the hours in classrooms, in libraries, on
buses on our way to work, before the new people we would
become: here we were, our dusty feet, chipped polish like
exotic scales, the concession stand with its sticky floor under
our flip flops, so real, so full of smells and music – *The Byrds,
Dylan, the Rolling Stones* – that we did not notice our fate
playing out in that living room with its piano, its portrait
of dead parents, the fireplace just before the brimming glitter
of wings.

The Birds, 1963

The view is wide, unploughed fields along fields of corn, ordered
  by a road
by telephone poles, fences – for most of its existence this would
  be the scene:
an emptiness, silence beneath the scorching sky

but then his bus grunts into view, stops, deposits him roadside,
  beside the ditch
we wait with him, nothing happens again and again, until a car
  approaches
lingers, zooms off leaving dirt in the air, in his eye, and again
time lengthens away like the road

Still we stay transfixed and know something is coming
taut with conjecture, alert and feeling the suspense as preamble
we wait for that alive instant that frees us from stasis

A few moments later a man finds his way to the opposite side of
  the road
We see them stand and stare at each other, we see the tight
  perspective
the highway stretching away into a controlled horizon

When we see this configuration again, it will be when he meets
  Eve in the woods
he will be on one side of the screen, she on the other, straight
  trees between them –
but then it will be love he is hounding, he is circling, he is
  avoiding.

North by Northwest, 1959

1945/1965

I've seen this movie before, as a teenager
in the living room of the house where I grew
up, the TV inherited from my mother's spinster
aunt in a low cabinet. I lay on the chesterfield
a friend on the chair, my cats milling about
solemn as sharks in a tank

           That brilliant autumn day
the movie quieted us, the love, especially, his
ardent grasp of her on the train, her sensible
pushing him back into dreams, rimming the
fractured mind where images surfaced, clues
to pry apart

           It was 1965, twenty years
since that black and white world was imprinted
on the sticky celluloid of the past, a time I
remember yards growing dim on summer nights
streets lined with houses caught in that moment
of warm pink skies

           – Ah, but the love, how gay
it was, how skippy-happy wonderful
after the turn of the black gun pointed away
from us, its red aim, when she rested
her life in her love's warm palm and our young
hearts swelled, pure and blind.

                              Spellbound, 1945

On the train platform, she walks from us
the twist of ankle, the static black
hair, a clipped high-heeled strut
her plan perverse and focused
and because it is without love, just as
innocent

The sound of the mother descending
the stairs heard
in dreams, the blunt urge forward
her silhouette black against a
filtered light, the huge sound of
shoes scuffing wood
how much damage we wonder
can emanate from this single image
of a mother's retreat

Her saviour will pluck that festered
polyp from the web of her past
will turn the wild blonde woman
she has become into the child
crouched on the stairs, stretching
back into those cruel years
of gladiolas fanned before windows
red frills tucked in green palms

What does he leave in place of her psychosis?
his grinding body above her? the narrowness
of his view, lust for the damaged beauty
she spread over the rooms of his wealth
like sunlight on walls: health and redemption
left, if you stop the moment here, on the veranda
looking toward the weak light by the harbour
after the storm with its pink distance –
if we don't let the years crowd in with
their disease and omens and wounds
she would be cured and empty of malice
but do not be fooled, this pain is a long
needle that pierces deep the heart
and stays hidden until a dull morning wakens
it, when she will lay anesthetized
as the wide spectrum of that destitute sky

Marnie, 1964

BIRDS

their wings dip blue
arcs, the swing of intersecting
swoops dot the sliding
dimensions of sky

they are not flecks
to be ignored, avoided –
they are pinpricks of depth

each a closed black fist
a philosopher's heart beating
true, stops to watch the lap by

the river's shore, the sticky
cumulus strings, a white mesh
over the land, and tiny us

roaming the quartered fields below them
they caw a greeting and know
all that will not
tame to words

The Birds, 1963

Paint cracked on shutters; windows open to the sad night –
there are only a few patterns, only so many new things
you get to see in your life, and only so far you can fall
from the innocence of your arrival, before you realize the knives
glinting cruelly in the dark all correspond somehow to the dark
space you brought with you; and there are only so many
nightmares before you notice the rhythms, the loop of images
the fear at that moment before the epiphany –

I'm thinking this because of the mother sitting on the veranda –
a late spring night, the lamps along the street so bright they glow
with a spiked light – she sits under the porch lamp, knitting
and dreaming something so mesmerizing that she hums as a way
to keep grounded in that chair, on that porch, in the year 1948.

Bruno waits on the bench, sees Marion with her two galoots
bound across the street to the bus, frantic as chiffon in wind;
    there's
laughter and cavorting – and here's the point where we must
stop, quiet our thoughts – the mother is left to finish her knitting
in the swampy air of that early summer night and we know at some
point later that evening, a stranger will mount those steps

to tell her of the murder and a new sense will invade that simple
struggling house, on that simple street in that struggling
    neighbourhood
and later still she will think, for the first time, that death – her own
certainly – is the only thing that still makes perfect sense.

Strangers on a Train, 1951

The smudge of decades blends with the fog of a London street
celluloid frays the gauzed sky into smoke and transports us
   to the
dim room caught in a 1920 light; through the blur of the
   sepia film

another history emerges, muted as smeared charcoal – look
closely, can you see where the fog ends and his cape begins?
where the lane moves into the landscape of his staged
   martyrdom

The distraught parents in rooms downstairs, comic and
   uncertain
and always wrong, and the villagers faceless in their cruelty
stuff the screen with grey images and a bleak distancing

But then we glimpse her and as sunlight breaks through
the clumped clouds of an abandoned sky, her laugh reaches us –
a stream of light from a distant star
            The Lodger: A Story of the London Fog, 1926

The German grunts as he rows at the front of the boat –
the minions with their tiny concerns scurrying
beneath him. He is the vicious sun, the unloving
father. They each know and fear his competence
which led them on that ill-fated voyage, deeper
and deeper into the maelstrom at the heart of
nothing, at the heart of that continuous, familiar
identical landscape of sea, sea, and still more sea
the curse of its endlessness, waves marked by
the diamond touch of sun or moonlight, the past fades
to a mirage beyond the blurred horizons.

Lifeboat, 1944

I've been there, by that bridge, by the lighthouse on Point Reyes
I've seen days like that, starkly bright, when the hills are burnt
and faded from the sun.
I know the smell of oysters by San Francisco Bay
and understand what he was after: a sense of mystery
the promise of love, a certain redemption
as full of regret as any childhood
for all life ends and here he shows us what is lost:
the cool air of those California nights, the lights in the marina
the sedate afternoon under the clever sky
lost in the delirium of betrayal.

Vertigo, 1958

It's hard to kill a man, difficult to trap
even that stupid one in the peasant kitchen
with its low ceiling. Beyond, spring fields
move out into acres of roving crops

Stuck in that godless light, pale on walls, the
last gasp, a crucifix of agony, we feel the pull
to earth, the snap back to the room where
escape is impossible, repulsed by his dirty

death; yet was he not once a child, in classrooms
in concrete yards, a sterile wind slapping
his trusting face, was he not once a boy in love
with a story of the past, now lost, and is this not

why we witness in sad silence his stubborn
reluctant, last impulse – a fierce "no"

Torn Curtain, 1966

The coast ablaze, an unfurling of primal light
I squint against its painful algebra
its continents of logic, and zip
the ragged, cliff-edged road

to reach the seaside town by
the bay where all is still, a
reprieve, the restaurant calm
the view constant, the pinot gris a bitter
pinch on my tongue

inland, off the town's main street
the schoolhouse stands brilliant in a
buzzing field of hot insects and stiff
weeds; fifty years ago, the same street,
same blaze of sun, the same blistering

mystery of want and worship, moving
out through the town drenched in the past
through the algorithm of shoreline, out to
the whipped eternity, an ocean of worth

The Birds, 1963

OLD MISSION, SAN JUAN BAUTISTA

From the roof he is a speck – his skull
smaller still – inside its small bowl, the image

of her a mass of electrons   firing like fireworks like
sparks fly   from a live electrical cable

dangerous stars

telling us all that the world
always ends   in chaos

even if we die quietly, those electrons
grow frantic   as ants searching for a home
a receptor – lost and frenzied and unforgiving

And this is the point:
no one survives
without the pang of old regrets, embers burning pure

at the core   the pain red, known by the heart's
palm   his worship scars deep

as the light of day fades   along the walkway
that laconic landscape   the chapel's serene arches

Vertigo, 1958

He was a smarty-pants, with his theories
and opinions, and intelligent calm
and the boy, a mini smarty-pants
we followed him, agreeing with

everything he did, said, every gesture
even as we wished he'd think of some
way to stop Doris's voice reaching
those octaves of distress –

but he was kind, no slaps
no *shut-up, for God's sake, let me think*
it was what he was there for –
the thinking part, and what she was
there for – the fretting part, a mother's
anguish imbuing every clenched utterance

Years later in a small house they each
have a room dedicated to their role, where
the longed-for, slippered moment of
his privilege and her singing in the kitchen
coalesce into a blind, suffocating harmony

The Man Who Knew Too Much, 1956

You're in my country now, and what do you see?
the same intrigues, faithless women and eager men
the same as anywhere, but where is the snow, Hitch
where's the winter? you could have done something with
that, forced a gang of interlopers to stay in a lodge
watching a storm rage, the Canadian version of a lifeboat
each with their plan of revenge and cold, cold survival

But no, instead you bring us to a church, drown us
in Montgomery's intense stare and take us into the
alleyways where love and evil intertwine and are dismissed
by the clamouring villagers, peasant solid, slack-jawed,
with weapons and a vacuous space behind their eyes.
It could be anywhere, you say, anywhere
where men and women mix, where there are streets
and parks and quiet waiting in cars, and where the
sky domes over the intrigue with its sense of the eternal

I Confess, 1953

twisted leaves gather dry   on the autumn
pathway   meandering to the asylum –
elsewhere war rages – everyone seems grown up

and so much death that tales seem drained of blood
there's a sameness to the grief – innocuous as
the grey of old clouds

she tells him there are answers that shy away
from his reach – she says, *there is one way to think
one final door opening in on the truth*
but from here   from this sardonic, content place
we know there is no such easy cure   and only

the search is true –   still how
grateful we are for her earnest talk, for
the way she holds his tormented head,   and speaks
sure, an incantation against
the diminishing light of all that remains   dead

Spellbound, 1945

That he's your relative makes it worse
you spend time thinking about this and
so do we – watching the shadow on the ceiling
of your sister's room as she sleeps
and the night settles weary on the house –
does he share more than a name, you wonder
the love of your doltish mother, certainly
but let's not forget the world you lived in
a world where children in other countries
were being rounded up and evil burned
bright, while you, caught in the simple, tiny
tyranny of his horrid waltz, cannot see
the pink stained clouds gathering
or the men in uniforms marching
you do not know how each mind is a letter
of a word, each word a promise broken.

Shadow of a Doubt, 1943

THE BACK LOT

Stacked with scenery on pulleys, wardrobes
stuffed with gowns and satin shoes, where her
feet suffered, solemn as salmon, and as dumb
the dresses spilling out from the rack, as
grapes tumble from the vine, her grey

suit on a hanger, its silvery aura muted, unburdened
by significance, the desolate clutter from those rooms
common with dust, abandoned to smoulder

in this surviving time, but there was a moment
years ago, when the combination of character
and setting and 1950 decorum crowded the sky
over the bridge, when rooms were orchestrated, clothes
pinned in place, and actors thrashed out their

story of pining silence, the crash of waves on a blonde
shoreline, dulled to this jumble of breakable things, made
resilient, more solid than those dead players, the quiet
of his car as he followed her, and the vertigo
that made their damaged love dizzy and inexplicable

Vertigo, 1958

ALMA AND ALFRED

After Hitch died, she stayed in her room
and spoke to him through the wall –
film threaded her mind's
dark projector – here an image of
a blonde in high heels before
the mist of the California
shore and there beneath the bed
a forgotten splatter of blood –
she'd ask about the lighting,
the mood, who was mad, who in love
and the stories crammed
and mutated in her mind
humming on in their infamy
like the woman in the upstairs
bedroom, infirm, evil and complicit,
the rocking woman who calls out to her
wayward son, lost in the swamp
beneath the pierce of the bird's cry.

                              Psycho, 1960

Autumn 1960, the Capital Theatre, Ottawa

In the lobby were life-sized cut-outs of Hitchcock –
a warning sounded that you could not enter the theatre
after the movie started. My mother and oldest brother
were in the crowd waiting. I was too young but I
wanted to be with them, to see the wolf
waiting in the dark, the mud caked
to his claws.

When they came home, I was waiting. They would only
say I was too young, my mother said it
with concern, my brother with glee. When she left
the room, he said: *there's a scene where the sister
hides in the stairwell leading to the fruit cellar
and just before she turns to leave, she sees a light
on below her,* my eyes widen, hands clutch the
chesterfield arm, *but then here comes the part you're
too young to know.* He laughed, turned away
and I hated him, hated once again the childhood that kept
everything worth knowing hidden

Summer 1969, Overbrook, Ottawa

The first time I saw *Psycho* was on TV in the
living room of my home, Patsy
and I watched it, *it's not so bad*, she said
until the shower scene, I hid my eyes
by folding my knees to my forehead

and refused to look until the music quieted
when I saw the perfect eye, a perfect
drain. We spent the next ten minutes
wondering how Marion would come back
and by the time we realized she would not
we were in a new world where we chased
the rickety plot that drove off like a runaway
train and left us by the side of the swamp
watching the winch and hitch lift her car
back into daylight.

1976, Carleton University, Film Studies 100

I'm taking notes in the darkened
auditorium, light from the lobby falls on my
workbook, I write: *change from white bra to
black – significance?* I watch the wash
of street lights on Marion's face and know
what she is driving toward: the motel
with the stuffed birds in mid-flight, the
darkness she disturbs, the swamp where she
will be submerged in a car trunk – after,
we go to the pub for a beer and laugh away
the desolate mood, the half-heard wolf howl

this was before the marriage, our small
apartment, the surprising turn of a life into
moments in offices, on buses, that sluggishly
moved through suburban streets, through
the myriad of complex seasons, and hope.

Halloween 1989, home: Burfield Ave.

I turned the TV on in the kitchen after
trick-or-treating with my stepson, and
there she is again, again the face of the police
filling the car window, and I want to warn her
do not go to that motel in the rain, do not veer
away from the main highway
and find those sorry rooms of winged
shadows, *I think you should change the channel*
my husband says, *he's too young to see this.*

Home, 2018

I've come to like the silence in the car
as I've come to like the car
silence in *Vertigo*, but here it is in black and
white and the people are poor. I know these
people, I've sat on buses with them and I know
the 1950s here, know the glint in the wolf's
eye. This was the era I was plunked into,
this the adulthood I anticipated: an office
on a hot day, high heels and tight skirt hemming
me in, my mind humming along to the twitch
of fluorescent light, until I raise my head and see him
so that later there will be a private moment
in a dusty hotel where
who I truly am is finally let loose.

Psycho, 1960

THE WOLF IN THE BASEMENT

when I was young I dreamt of a wolf in our basement
like the wolves sighted in the fields surrounding our home

I told my mother who told me to play outside – there
in the muddy backyard, the untamed streets. My father
was alive then, sick with the illness that claimed him, and she
– listening for the retch of this illness – could not care

about my wolf. And so he stayed there, gleaming silver
and silent in the long platinum strands of moonlight

until your different wolf appeared and woke mine
and I felt his restless roaming beneath me – in movie
theatres, in living rooms, where the grumble of the wolf's
dark wisdom was heard over the grumble of those actors

he is there still, in the coal bin – his tail's gentle sway
as he looks up the stairway to the kitchen where the years
played out, a wolf illuminated in the yellow glow of morning

in the stark white of a fading afternoon and in the repeated
slump of days into thousands of nights.

NOTES AND ACKNOWLEDGMENTS

"Bel Air, 1980," "A Story of the London Fog," "The View from Point Reyes," and "Alma and Alfred" were published in *A Sea of Alone: Poems for Alfred Hitchcock*, edited by Christopher Conlon (Smith Point, New York: Dark Scribe Press, 2011). "Drive-in, 1969" was published in *I Found It at the Movies: An Anthology of Film Poems,* edited by Ruth Roach Pierson (Guernica Editions, 2014). "Drive-in" was published in issue #71 of *Magma* (UK), Summer 2018. My thanks to the editors of these publications.

I wish to extend a special thanks to my writing friends Frances Boyle (who would not let me give up on my different wolf), Laurie Koensgen, Jean Van Loon, Lise Rochefort, Jacqueline Bourque, Sonia Tilson, Claudia Radmore, Ian Colford, Rhonda Douglas, and the wonderful poets who are part of the poetry group The Ruby Tuesdays.

I also would like to thank Kimmy Beach for her expert tutelage and careful reading of these poems, and Isabel Huggan, whose pronouncement of "brilliant" at the very beginning of this odyssey sustained and validated my effort throughout.

To the kind souls at McGill-Queen's University Press, and in particular my editor, Allan Hepburn, I am indebted for their insight and empathetic reading of this book.

To my friends and family, I send my love and appreciation for all they have done to support me during the creation of this collection.

And once again, and always, my gratitude and love to André Savary.